WARNING

CHIEF APOSTLE RAY

JIM JONES? JONESTOWN? "ALARMING SIMILARITIES"

Thomas Vick

INKS & BINDINGS

Inks and Bindings
888-290-5218
www.inksandbindings.com
orders@inksandbindings.com

Contents

1
JIM JONES

Who was Jim Jones? And who is this Ray individual, who claims to be the best human being that has ever lived and calls himself the Chief Apostle? Ironically, they both have a lot of Alarming Similarities. However, these statements should be near the end of the book instead of in the first three sentences. Therefore, we must start from the beginning of who each individual is. Let us first remember who Jim Jones was in this chapter.

James Warren Jones was born May 13, 1931 in the small town of Crete, which is near Lynn, Indiana. Many people that knew him as a child mentioned that he was very strange. He sometimes had the urge to display control issues against his friends or children that would dare to associate with him. He once locked his "friends" in the barn. He was obsessed with viewing death, as he did one time when he attentively watched a cat die by killing it with a knife. He was fascinated with the deeds of Adolf Hitler.

Ironically, he became a regular church goer. He graduated from an Indianapolis college in 1961. However, before graduation, he had already started to get a following in the early 1950's. By 1955 it was called the "Peoples Temple", all in the Indianapolis area. He claimed he had special powers and one of those most prominent claims was that he could foretell the future. One prediction that did not happen, was that there would be a nuclear attack on U.S. Soil on July 15, 1967. That prediction was the propellant that was needed to make his followers flee to northern California, in the Redwood Valley.

His prediction didn't happen, so it was time to move south to San Francisco. During this time in California he received a title, "The Prophet"! To get a title with that magnitude gave him the zeal to control his followers even more. There were accusations that he was illegally acquiring the income or assets of many of his followers. Because the investigations of these allegations started, it was necessary for Jim Jones to flee with his followers to South America.

So, in 1977, the cult fled to Guyana, which is east of Venezuela. There the compound of nearly a thousand people made their final move. The allegations were made that many did not want to move but were forced with threats

2

and possibly physical abuse. One couple had a child while they were part of the movement and the boy was placed in the home of Jim Jones. Miraculously the couple escaped from moving to the southern continent. The child ended up there though, and became one of the deceased later. Complaints were filed and a Congressman Leo Ryan got involved to investigate. Several other complaints included that many of the cult members were held against their will at the compound.

Congressman Leo Ryan with several reporters and other important people flew to that remote compound a few days before November 18th. However, on that date, November 18, 1978, the chain of events that made history began. The investigation group which was led by the congressman returned to the airport from the compound, along with several of the members of the cult that wanted to leave. When they arrived at the airport and waiting for the plane, the militia force from Jim Jones also arrived and opened gun fire upon them. The congressman and four of his team, plus several of the fleeing cult members died during that assault.

At the compound Jim Jones knew he had to do the unthinkable immediately. There are opposing views of whether Jim Jones murdered many of them, or if all of the members did suicide of their own free will. He had made a cyanide infused drink with Flavor-Aid, and not Kool-Aid like so often mentioned. He supposedly ordered the children

3

to drink first and then everyone else. Somewhere, around 913 to possibly 918 people died that day by the actions of one very deranged man. Records stated that 304 of the dead were children. Just a few of their members escaped the tragedy. Some were simply not at the compound when everything started to go insane.

There is one conflicting idea. Some say Jim Jones after committing this horrific act committed suicide by a shot to his head. Another belief is that his nurse, Anne Moore, shot him so that he couldn't escape his deserved fate, and then she shot herself. Regardless how it ended, Jim Jones died at a young age of 47.

When talking to survivors that had family members die in that catastrophe, they cringe at the sound of the people that sort of joke with the phrase, "They drank the Kool-Aid"!

2
Origin of the COGR

Danny Layne grew up in a conservative church. However, he took to illegal drugs and soon was a heroin addict living on the streets of California. He claimed he had destroyed nearly every vein by injecting the poison into his body for nineteen years. Another claim he had was that he tried committing suicide with a meat cleaver by slashing his wrists. The irony was that when he hit the bottom of not even wanting to live, he said he found religion and God again.

Because he had such a remarkable or maybe even eccentric conversion, he started getting a following around the 1980's and 1990's. Quite often you would hear people mention the Danny Layne movement. At the time he was attending one of the many Church of God congregations. We need to address the issue of the name of a church.

Somebody mentioned that there are about eight million people that claim they belong to that name of Church affiliation. However, there are a multitude of divisions or branches of faith, with totally different beliefs and practices under the same name. Therefore, many use an additional name or location after the Church of God name. Danny's group after they split away from a conservative church named themselves the Church of God Restoration. They started preaching and testifying that they are restoring true religion. All other churches are wrong, even if they use the name Church of God. They preached that they were the only true church and everyone else was Babylon.

Danny was very extreme compared to typical beliefs or practices. Almost any activity that a normal family or person would enjoy, he condemned it. There was a book published several years ago by a man named Bernie, who titled his book, "Torn asunder in the jaws of a cult". He was once a member of the Danny Layne movement and extensively wrote about many of the condemned activities or items. Some of the most fanatical was the beating of their children for discipline. There were many bruised children among that group during those years. There was a woman in the congregation that used to be a nurse before joining that group. Sue told parents that if they beat their children the way this church teaches, that they are to quickly soak their child in Epsom salt to eliminate the bruising sooner.

They also taught against any medical attention, meaning you don't go to doctors nor take any medicine. You simply trust in God. There were two brothers one time that joined up with this fanatical Danny Layne. The names were Ray (the person this book is about) and Gerry. The three of them even went to Africa as a team to start a new church.

Gerry seemed to be the more level headed, analyzing things realistically. Unfortunately, he is the one that fell from a height unto concrete. This book which you are reading now only repeats what was written in the book previously mentioned. The fall and injury resulted in a hernia which became the size of a volleyball. No medicine or doctors were allowed during those days when Layne was the "King" of that movement. Ironically, they don't believe in doctors, but then Danny ordered a doctor procedure. Members were ordered to push the hernia back in. Imagine having your entire intestines inside this hernia ball in front of you! Several "brothers" tried doing the procedure. A blood vessel ruptured and he bled to death shortly after that! The preposterous claim later by members for the murder cover-up was that Gerry had heart trouble all his life. Would you have heart trouble if you had a hernia that size and was getting it pushed back in? Gerry died, leaving behind a wife and several children.

In his book, Bernie, elaborated on how TV and any motion on a computer was forbidden. We needed to install this last sentence here and it will be brought up again later in this book to see the change under this man named Ray. In some ways the group has gotten more normal, but in other areas it has become poisonous, and will be explained later.

It was peculiar that this former drug addict knew exactly the right amount of emotions in a church service. The group became fairly loud in song service and during the preaching. If there was a group louder than this Restoration, they were condemned and labeled as having a devilish spirit. On the other hand, if they didn't jump around like Danny Layne, they were considered spiritually dead. He referred to his past church as the Church of Frigidaire, "frigid-air.

This group's dress standard is extreme, and resembles the most conservative 1800's type of clothing. Women will wear dresses all time, down to their ankles. Men will always have long sleeves and the top collar button always shut. Every button has to be shut. The video I mentioned on the back cover of this book, with the "Rat" exposing some of their sermons, is what they look like all the time and not just at their church service. I have to modify that statement. The men will not wear suits when they are working at their profession or job, but will just be similar dressed without the suit coat.

The most disturbing thing about this congregation is how they have split up MANY marriages. A congregation in Warsaw, Indiana, under the pastor who is second after Ray, split up half the marriages in that congregation while he was the pastor. His name is Steve, and he was the individual that served the "Key Lie Pie" in the Rat U-Tube video. That pastor moved down to Muncie and is in the process of deceiving the community with twisted religion down there.

One individual that is constantly exposing this movement has a website, *cultbusters.us*. His name is Adam who also lost his wife and family into this cult. Usually when a member of this evil movement leaves or gets kicked out, they go totally the opposite direction spiritually. Most of them give up on religion all together and live a life that is far from what God would have for them. It is far and few people that actually survive the constant assault of cult pressures after they leave, but then even more rare an individual that keeps fighting to expose the evil that goes on in that place. It is not only on a spiritual realm of deception, but also allegations that has taken members to jail for sexual misconduct of minors. Ray was warned earlier of this behavior of a man and did nothing. This close affiliate to Ray is presently in Prison for a long sentence.

But we are getting too far ahead for this particular chapter. Danny Layne died and Ray became the new "King" for the group. That is when a lot of changes happened. The ministers decided to elect twelve of their pastors to get the inflated title, "Apostle"! And Ray received the greatest title. He is regarded to be the Chief Apostle Ray. He supposedly, according to their group, is the best man that ever lived. In a court setting, accusing someone of something holds just a few ounces of persuasion. However, getting the defendant on video saying the same thing is what is needed to seal the conviction for the jury. Therefore, if you haven't gone to _cultbusters.us_ or looked up the U-Tube video, _Get Your Spiritual Rat Poison_ then it will be hard for you to actually see the evidence of evil. Evil we say? What evil are we talking about? Let us analyze good food, dirty food, and finally poisoned food in the next chapter.

3

Good corn & oats?

Since we can't visually demonstrate the point that we will try to make in this chapter, you will need to turn on your imagination skills. Start imagining driving to a feed store for cattle or even feeding the wildlife. You buy a hundred-pound bag of feed, which is made up of good corn and oats or such. Once you have it back home you dump the contents out on a table. It is best if it had been ground up into powder instead of whole kernels of corn. Intact corn kernels sometime do not get digested or utilized while going through the many parts of the digestive system. Therefore, cracked corn or ground meal is a lot more efficient feed.

While on the table you look at it. You can smell it and even taste it. It is good feed for any critter that wants it. But now let us take some thistles, a few stones, and a handful of dirt and stir it into and throughout this pile of feed on your table. Is it edible and will the animals eat it? Sure, they will but might leave some of it behind that has a greater amount of dirt mingled into it. The stones will remain on the table also. But the cattle or other animals will not die.

But what if you were evil or had a cause to exterminate a specific creature. Take good high-quality feed and take a highly toxic poison and use a spray bottle for the next step. Turn the nozzle to the mist position and sparingly spray a fine mist, amounting to less than a teaspoon, onto this large pile of feed. Stir it around well and you have feed that will kill anything that will eat it.

This chapter basically expounds on the brilliant U-Tube rat video already mentioned. Whoever put that together made a good point. Rat poison has a lot less poison in it then this formula or recipe that was just given to you. One teaspoon of poison for every one hundred pounds of feed is an extremely potent concoction compared to what is needed to kill. Humans are not that different than rats in the sense of what they focus on. Both humans and rats focus on all that good corn and oats! With that much good in proportion, how can the food not be any good?

It is such a microscopic amount of poison, that the mice and rats can't detect it and therefore die. The small amount of cyanide in the Flavor-Aid probably wasn't even tasted by anyone. And spiritual poisoning can be just as easily missed if the victims are focusing on the good corn and oats. Long term victims often are by then under the influence of blind obedience, that they don't even test the food they are receiving against the Word of God. The Bible is dismissed if the Chief Apostle Ray made a statement which is contrary to scripture. "But Ray preaches so well", they might say.

I will include other resources that I haven't already mentioned. But if you analyze with the thought of convincing a jury, the most important or gravitating content is video made from this fanatical group themselves. The rat video is good or alright, but the inserts are priceless. There is a much longer video that has priceless video clips in it which you can find on *cultbuster.us*. It is titled, "The Jesus Replaced Church". The man that made it has too much insignificant information in it, and rambles on for an entire hour. I wish he would have drastically shortened it, or split it up into three or four videos. However, the spliced in videos are what convinces me that this movement is a cult. It is loaded with spiritual cyanide or strychnine.

What is the difference between spiritual dirt versus spiritual poison. Members of the cult might argue with people like Adam, who has the website. "Why don't you attack other churches instead of ours?" "Certain churches have pastors molesting children." "Some churches preach false doctrines." "So why do you constantly bash us?"

13

To answer those questions, we must have you turn on your imagination again. The church setting includes the building, the ministry, and the people. We will call that the "church" and imagine it to represent the good corn and oats. We need to now throw out some examples without becoming a sermon of a certain faith. There are four gospels: Matthew, Mark, Luke, and John. Just before getting crucified, Jesus had a certain colored robe put on him. Read each gospel and notice a difference of opinion. Is it a contradiction of the Bible? Do a test among people you meet. Take an "Aqua" colored sheet of paper, and ask people what color it is. Some might say green. Some might say blue. Some might even say it is aqua, or blue-green. The four gospel writers saw the color from a different perspective. If a modern-day church argues about which color was the correct color, is that poison? It isn't any more than dirt.

Some congregations believe that the nails were driven into Jesus's hands like the Bible says. Other congregations say that during Jesus's time, the hands included the wrists, which would hold the body on the cross better than in the palm of the hand. Is either opinion, poisonous? No! Is one of the opinions possibly, "dirt"? Once again, I would say no. At worst, I could possibly say that one of them might have a rock pebble in their good corn and oats. But neither view is poisonous!

14

What if the pastor had an affair with a child? Is that a poisonous church? Did the pastor condone or preach that such affairs are normal or Biblical? If they did, then it could be spiritual poison in that church. It is basically sinful behavior in that congregation. So, fighting against churches that have dirt in their weekly spiritual menu would be somewhat a microscopic problem compared to a poison infested menu. The next chapter will be addressed to the many examples of a Spiritually Poisonous menu of this Chief Apostle Ray church. The examples must be contrary to scripture or a robbing of the deity of Jesus Christ or God, to be considered spiritually poisonous.

4

Spiritual Poison

Let us analyze each insert made in the two videos mentioned. First, we will dissect the rat video and throw away everything but the videos of the group themselves. Jesus spoke these words. "Come unto me, all ye that labour and are heavy laden, and I will give you rest." Matthew 11:28

In the first insert, the Chief Apostle Ray Tinsman, hijacked the basic words of Jesus and applied the words to himself. The listener is supposed to follow him, and get behind him. Are not Christians supposed to follow Christ and get behind him? There was a real apostle (not this group's fake) in the New Testament that said, "Follow me, only as I follow Christ"? But here Ray leaves the ending, of following Jesus out. If he did this by innocence, why did he acknowledge this "poison", by saying, "There, I said it!"

16

It appears that he knew he was stealing the words of Jesus, and placing the demand to "be followed" upon himself. That is an example of taking the deity from Christ and placing it upon himself. It is spiritual poison and the members, or should we say victims, in this group can't see it.

The Bible says that there, "are none righteous, no not one." "All have sinned and come short of the glory of God." Once again, ministers of this group are practically worshipping this man, Ray Tinsman! The minister called him a perfect man! Now a comment like that, is it dirty, full of nasty debris, or is it actually poison? Members of this cult don't even look at all the scriptures this statement contradicts. Even words of Jesus are eliminated to claim that this human being is equal to Jesus who lived a perfect life. Serious souls in that place should have gotten up and ran out the door when they heard this blasphemous comment. That statement is poison, and they continue drinking or eating it!

The Bible mentions that when we are Christians, that we have the Holy Spirit and Jesus to intercede for us. According to this cult you would have to surmise that Jesus must be still dead. They didn't mention much about the Holy Spirit as a mediator. They acknowledge that we need to reach out to God. But the error comes in when we pray to Jesus. We are wrong supposedly when we pray to Jesus! Ray, in the third insert claims that praying to Jesus is weird stuff! However, one minister started praying in the name

17

of Ray, their Chief Apostle, and he claims the heavens opened to him! This is another example of spiritual poison and blasphemous!

Do you know this man in Ohio or Indiana, called Ray? According to their teaching on insert number four, you better find him if you want to go to heaven. He must measure you to see if you are spiritually fit to get there! No longer is salvation in Jesus Christ acceptable and a guarantee for eternal bliss, but you better stoop to a carnally controlled and power-seeking Ray. You must get permission from him to enter heaven! In Acts, God added to his Church daily as he saw fit. This cult took the power away from God, and gave that power to Ray to add to the church as he sees fit! Another blasphemous comment, and very poisonous!

In, The Jesus Replaced Church, video, the long-winded speaker addressed the situation with what happened in the Book of Acts. A man, named Cornelius tried to worship an Apostle, and bowed down before him. The Apostle picked him up, and admonished him to not worship him, claiming he is a man also. However, in insert five, this minister only used the first half of that situation. In his context, he saw it righteous to worship, and bow before their Chief Apostle Ray. His story ends there, which is contradictory to what happened in scripture. Do you think worshipping another human being is just "dirty corn and oats"? Or is there a poison floating throughout that congregation?

18

There were many Apostles and prophets throughout history and the Bible. Peter and Paul healed the sick and even brought the dead back to life! Many miracles were performed by men and even in the Old Testament. Elisha or Elijah raised up a boy that had died. Moses was used by God to do the ten plagues and then parting the Red Sea. There are so many miracles by people that God had called for his messengers. However, today lives a man that has never done a single unexplained miracle. He can't heal the blind, the lame, or the dead. But the claim is that he is better than ALL the other people that has ever lived, except Jesus Christ! Notice how they don't acknowledge Jesus as the Son of God, but call him, the "man" Jesus Christ. Jesus was just a man to this cult!

The only accomplishment that Ray did is gather a couple thousand people together that are loyal to him, similar to what Jim Jones did. No super natural powers, no healing has he done. He didn't even have the power over the courts to keep the child molester from going to prison. He was there when his brother died of the huge hernia. Where is his power, or special calling of God. Could you call him the Chief of all the Prophets or Apostles?

Before Jesus left this Earth, he said that if you are his true disciple (established), greater works than Jesus will he do. The early Apostles did that! But Ray hasn't! If Ray is the Chief Apostle, then Jesus must be a liar for saying that (real apostles) would do greater miracles! My thoughts are that Jesus is true, and every man contrary to him is a liar! Can you see the spiritual cyanide that this group is drinking?

In this life there are heroes that jump into a burning house or flooded rivers to save an individual. It is righteous to admit that if it hadn't been for the hero, that the other person would have died. They owe their life to that hero. But when a preacher claims other facets of his being, which should be attributed to another human being, it is dangerous. His life could be saved by another person. However, God gave each person a soul. Nobody can take that soul away from you. Nobody has given it to you except God. Salvation only comes through Jesus Christ by the price he paid at Calvary.

The number seven insert is one of the greatest blasphemous comments made. The preacher claims, "I owe my life, I owe my soul, I owe my salvation to one man..." How long did Ray hang on the cross for the sins of that pastor? It is so horrific of a statement, and the cyanide drinkers still remain in this poisonous group. Look at all the good corn and oats! Ray must have a lot of good tasting Flavor-Aid punch for his victims to keep drinking. The Bible in Second Thessalonians mentions that if you get prompted by the Holy Spirit of some false information, but you override it, God will eventually allow you to be so deceived that you willingly believe a lie. Many of the people in that group are in that state already.

There are women that were appointed to be in the group of twelve Apostles. There was a man dying in their congregation a few years ago. All twelve of their Apostles probably prayed for the healing of this sick man, Dietrich. How can all these apostles, including this Chief Apostle, who is supposedly better than all the previous apostles, not heal him? If Apostle Peter would have been on the scene, I'm sure he would have raised him up. Ironically, Ray is supposed to be better than Apostle Peter.

Soon it appeared Dietrich was on his death bed. Apostle Elizabeth claimed she had a vision from God. She claimed that God told her that he would be a liar if he didn't allow their apostles to heal him. Even if he died, God would allow these Apostles to raise him back to life. Ironically, Dietrich died and remained dead! Listen to insert number eight which is much more convincing than my feeble attempt at writing of the dangers in this group.

In the Old Testament, Elizabeth would have been considered a false prophet, and she would have been stoned to death. However, members that are caught up in this cult, will defend her. They might bring up Lazarus. Did Jesus heal him? Certainly, but he is still dead. Accusations fly, and they might say that you weren't there, how do you know he wasn't healed but died after that? Round and round it goes with circular reasoning, when they deliberately choose to belief a lie. Many were the people that believed that the

Flavor-Aid was the best thing for them and they stayed in their circumstance, and then died. For Jim Jones followers it was a physical death. For this cult we are talking about a spiritual death. They have put their salvation in a man, instead of Jesus Christ.

The ninth insert goes along with that thought. The preacher claims there will come a day when people will just have to say, "I want to be with you (cult), and they will be sealed". No Jesus Christ needed, no cross, no repentance, and no salvation needed! Just join this group and say "yes", to their Chief Apostle Ray! Totally throw the Bible away! It is not needed anymore. Blasphemous and spiritual poison! Unfathomable that the members can't see the truth. God must have blinded their eyes.

In the second video that I mentioned (The Jesus Replaced Church), just take the one excerpt where the man is preaching about Christianity. Christianity was used by the early Christians in the Book of Acts. If you followed the teachings of Jesus Christ, you were called a Christian, and with the constantly growing numbers it became known as Christianity! But here in this excerpt, Apostle Patrick Jr. preached that the problem with churches today is the Christians and Christianity! He preached, "We are not Christianity! We are Layne-ites!" As in Danny Layne, who supposedly founded or started this group. The man that was a heroin addict for 19 years and burnt a lot of his brain out! They are attached to him and not to Jesus Christ. How much evidence does the jury need when they are so blunt of denying the Christian faith and simply following a man? They are Layne-ites ruled under the Chief Apostle Ray, who they say is a "perfect" man. Really?

And then Steve Hargrave, the second in power, talks in the video about lying. All this above information in this chapter, is directly video documented, where their preachers are doing all the talking. The rat didn't say a word, but all the inserts are priceless. They are excerpts from their ministers doing all the speaking. And yet Steve is lying about video makers that are supposedly making up things that are not true. He is accusing the video makers of lying and yet their preaching confirms the accusations of the makers. Doesn't that make Steve the liar?

That man has devised a plan of infiltrating his fanatical teachings into the Muncie area. He started an outreach for younger children to attend a "boot camp" with certain activities. It will mostly be fun and games at first. It will all be just good corn and oats. If it only went that far, it would be alright. But knowing the track record of what goes on in this group, it should alarm the parents to watch for advances of the cyanide. They might eventually bring in their religious beliefs. It maybe will still be the good clean feed. However, it might just be a short time before the poisoning begins. I urgently stress that you need to watch both videos to get the impact of who they are. If you dismissed all the information written by ex-members, and even the things I'm writing now, but looked at the cult's preaching, you would see the dangers.

5

Shifting Sand

In chapter two, I brought up the origin of this cult. It was under the control of Danny Layne. There was one sentence I wrote about any motion on the computer or TV was forbidden at the time. Danny died and Ray became the chief now. That is when things, beliefs, and concepts started changing like the ever-changing sand dunes. What they believed twenty years ago, might be obsolete today. They no longer preach against moving pictures. Many of their members have TVs in their homes. At least one congregation shut their church doors on a Sunday evening service, and instead went to a theater! That was the rumor I heard from a reliable source. If it is true, my accusation of shifting sand is accurate.

If you read the book written by a man that used to be in this cult, he outlines most of the things, or activities that used to be forbidden. He wrote about how he got in a mess when he wanted to take his children to an airshow. That activity was highly forbidden at the time. Many years later many of the cult members that condemned it went to airshows. His book, "*Torn Asunder in The Jaws Of A Cult*..." But like I mentioned before, I do not inhale everything that an ex-member writes. I feel they might have an ax to grind, because of how they were mistreated. I can feel the hurt of this man by his writing. It is good information but it isn't what I would depend on in a court setting. The man Adam also has a lot of important view points. He does a lot of narrating or clarifying what the cult does or teaches.

After Danny died, is when this cult decided to create twelve apostles. They needed to do that to somehow built their puzzle in a way that fits into the Bible spectrum. They couldn't choose eleven or thirteen apostles, because then it wouldn't image the various twelve elements. Twelve pillars or whatever, was the backdrop of what was needed. This was some of the sand that the wind blew into the recent scenery. Ray became the Chief Apostle. With twelve "pillars", more money was needed to support them. While searching through various writings, I read the rumor that they demand seven hundred and fifty thousand dollars per year, which is divided up to those apostles. Ray supposedly gets $150,000 a year!

That is a lot more money than a lot of common people make. Since churches do not get audited, a lot of that money could be distributed "under the table". Wondering if the church just pays the rent and items that Ray needs? Therefore, he has no income. If he got audited, what would they find? No income, even though living lavishly?

Some members (maybe all), were told to expose their finances to the ministry. They need to know how much you make and how much is your expense, and for what items. Some sermons declare that members don't need a nice house and they need to downsize and give the difference to the ministry. The money flow coming in and going out needs to be transparent to the leaders. That is some of the corrupt sand that blew into view in the last few years. Let us look at some Bible stories that would provide input of what is wrong here.

Remember Moses when he was called by God from the burning bush? He was ordered to help free God's people from their bondage in Egypt. Moses objected to that order because how was he supposed to convince the people and also Pharaoh? God told him to put his hand inside his clothing. He did, and then God told him to bring it back out. When Moses did, his hand was white with Leprosy! God ordered him to put his hand back into his clothing, and when he brought it back out, his hand was normal. God then told him to throw his rod down, and it turned into a snake. He was ordered to grab the snake by the tail, and it turned back into his rod.

When Moses dropped his rod or staff in front of Pharaoh, it turned into a snake again. The magicians or sorcerers could do the same and turned other rods into snakes. But Moses's rod or snake, ate all the other snakes. Then the ten plaques came and devastated Egypt. Without any of the miracles, would the children of Israel have been made free? Absolutely not, because there would not have been any display of God's supernatural and miraculous power.

I don't want to make this book long so I need to just mention that many prophets worked miracles, proving that they were chosen of God. Nobody could deny it. Eventually, Jesus started his short ministry with a lot of opposition. What ingredient was absolutely necessary to prove that he was chosen by God? I will insert exactly what it was by a scripture which Jesus spoke.

__"But if I do, though ye believe not me, believe the WORKS; that ye may know, and believe, that the Father is in me, and I in him."__ **John 10:38** It was the many miracles that Jesus did that proved he was sent by God. Healed the lame, the blind, the many diseases, and raised Lazarus from the dead. Nobody could say that he was a fake by the many supernatural powers from God.

Christ was crucified and rose again which gave birth to the Church, and the Apostles with boldness declared Jesus

Christ as the Lord. It was then that the real Apostles did many supernatural miracles as Jesus did because they were chosen by God. They worshipped Jesus as being Lord over all creation. They preached the truth and therefore God gave them Godly power to do the very WORKS that Jesus had done. They healed the sick, the blind, the crippled, and raised the dead. The community knew the Godly power they possessed, and they laid their sick in the street where they assumed the Apostles might walk by. They believed that the very shadow of these Apostles had power to heal. It was AFTER God gave these Apostles the miraculous healing power, that converts believed and sold their possessions and laid them at these God ordained Apostles. The riches didn't come first.

But this cult has it backwards. They are demanding all the revenue. And yet the ministry has no Godly connection, no supernatural Godly power to eject even a sliver. It's like putting the cart before the donkey! The cart is the free and eagerly willing flow of money from the newly saved. But the donkeys are not doing their part of demonstrating Godly power. All twelve donkeys couldn't save Dietrich nor any sickness. These twelve donkeys have no Godly power because they have eliminated the savior Jesus from his rightful place. They are not Christians nor Christianity by their own admission. They are Layne-ites as in Danny Layne that burnt his brain, and also had no Godly power.

He couldn't save Gerry with the hernia. He couldn't save the baby in his own congregation. I believe the real Apostle Peter could have because he was chosen by God. You don't need to fear these donkeys because they have no Godly power. They don't even have the Pharaoh's sorcerers' power which could do some miracles.

There is absolutely no proof like Moses had, like Jesus displayed, or like the real Apostles had, with these donkeys. There is absolutely no proof that they are even called by God. They are self-appointed and only say they are, what they claim they are. A big empty soap bubble of nothing.

"Verily, verily, I say unto you, He that believeth on me, the WORKS that I do shall he do also; and greater WORKS than these shall he do; because I go unto my Father. John 14:12

The reason these donkeys will NEVER have miracles, is the word (believeth) is missing in their doctrine and belief. They don't worship Jesus. If this group takes these lofty titles of "Apostles", and are absolutely without any demonstration of supernatural Godly power, they make Jesus a liar! The New Testament Apostles proved Jesus's words to be true. But these want-to-be apostles, are fakes and self-proclaimed. All Christians should have a Godly hatred for how they have trampled Jesus and his word into the dirt. First, they rate themselves better than Jesus, and then they usurp even God's righteous throne! God is supposed to be the Judge.

Since Ray became the "king", sermons have been preached that the entire world will be judged by Ray. He is the judge over everyone. Even Bill Gates will bow at the feet of Chief Apostle Ray to be judged! What blasphemous claims. Isn't Jesus the King of all kings, and God the Judge of all Judges. With those claims, they are in a very dangerous place spiritually. More blowing sand that is poisonous.

They are known for being a very misleading and a "vague answer" group. They might give a reply to your question, even though they didn't answer the question. Watch a long video made in Canada. Notice at the end of the presentation how Apostle Henry from Canada responded to a reporter. He gives a reply, but doesn't answer the question. The video, *Church of God Restoration Is A Cult // Theo Live – Episode 8*. It was recorded 2 years ago. You will notice many of the videos are repeated from the previous videos already mentioned. There are many new ones though.

One of the new clips is at a town meeting where Ray and Steve answered questions from the community of concerned citizens. One alarming reply to a question, was if this man Ray, could write scripture? Basically, if Ray didn't think the Bible was complete, could he write another addition to it? Watch that video to hear his answer. That also is poisonous sand that has blown into the scene. How can the members keep drinking this poison?

31

This is a short chapter and my mission is to make this a short book. I didn't want a full unabridged version of all the evil in this group. My mission for this book is to give you just a few points and directions for you to look into, and see if it creates an interest for you. There are other websites and sources that elaborate on this cult, but if the sources I provided don't move you, then another hundred wouldn't change anything.

6

Jim Jones & Ray Tinsman
Similarities

Both of these men have a lot of similarities. Ironically, they both started in Indiana. Ray, grew up near Farmland, Indiana. Both men were regular church goers. There might be a comparison of possibly having both of their choice of affiliation, being on the fringe of being a little bit eccentric. Jim started getting a following at a fairly young age. From what I gathered, it appears Ray started preaching when he was a teenager, possibly sixteen.

Jim Jones was known for a mixed racial group. If you watched the videos mentioned, you will see that this cult is a mixed racial group, with apostle Steve Hargrave supposedly the second in authority after the Chief apostle Ray.

Jim started in Indiana, moved to California to a few locations, and eventually ended up in South America. Ray has congregations in California, Canada, Mexico, and other countries around the world. The members all need to be in close proximity of each "church" building location. That was true for Jim who basically died at a compound. It is also true for members of Ray's cult. They need to live fairly close to each other.

Jim received the Huge Title of being the "Prophet". Ray received the Huge Title of the "Chief Apostle", the best man that EVER lived! Jim was and Ray is very arrogant. Both relish the praise of men. Both men believe they have supernatural power of knowing the future. Jim was proved wrong when there was no nuclear attack, and yet his members continued to blindly follow him. Ray also claims he has the book of Revelation all figured out. A few years ago, they had appointed twelve apostles that would reflect the mysteries of that last book of the Bible. But there is starting to be a rip in their theology with some of their apostles not towing the line that Ray has set. Apostle Henry seems to be the target recently. There are other issues that are germinating below the scenes at this time.

Both Jim and Ray have a gullible, blind and deceived followers. Each man had or presently has people within their group that wish they could get out and leave but are scared. The people that fled the Jim Jones compound, four of them were shot at the airport and died. The people that flee Ray's cult, get away and think they are free. However, they can't cope with the spiritual garbage that was embedded in their brain for so many years, concerning that this cult is the one true church. They quite often turn to drugs or other sins to silence the internal torment, or they sheepishly go back to the vomit they fled from. Rarely does an ex-member get stabilized in the Bible and gets spiritually firm.

The control both by Jim and Ray is by a lot of fear. Jim supposedly even had threats and possibly even physical pain brought upon members that wanted to leave. Ray has other tactics, and not just excommunication with shunning. Imagine being a child in Ray's cult with your entire family being part of it. You hate the system and when you turn eighteen, you leave. Your entire family will disown you, or they are supposed to. You were not allowed to have any friends outside of this congregation, so when you leave, you may not know anyone that you can turn to for help. There might be a time when you walk down a sidewalk, and you see ahead of you maybe your parents or other members of the cult coming toward you. Upon them seeing you, sermons were preached that the members need to immediately cross the street to avoid you. If anyone dies from the members of this cult, even if it is a close family member of yours, you will be banned from going to their funeral. This paragraph gives a partial definition of the term, shunning! Even if your intentions are not to leave the cult, any disagreement with the ministry will get a lot of reprove, and you will experience fear.

There was a man that was born in the late 1800's, that was quite eccentric like Jim Jones. That man died when Jim was living in California. Jim quickly went back to Indiana and deceived some of the members of the diseased man. It appears that maybe it was the wife of the diseased that saw what was happening and gave a loud response of Jim's actions. Jim even claimed he was their dead leader's reincarnation. Many believed his lies and fled Indiana, to California with Jim, when the "Woman" became loudly offensive verbally.

Ray and his cult members do the same thing. They call it going "Fishing" when they visit other congregations of different types and flavors. Their main purpose is not to worship together, but to sneak in and steal members whom they can convince and lure away. Cult members get told to get names and addresses while their apostle keeps the pastor of the other church occupied.

Jim Jones was accused of defrauding or embezzling money and assets from his members. This cult ruled by Ray who also tries to swindle and demand money from its members. You saw the video about the pressure put on a certain congregation to give thousands of dollars or they won't be saved. The coercion and high-pressure tactics to confiscate enough money for the ministry is disgusting!

When investigations started about illegal gains financially, Jim Jones fled to South America. Danny Layne received government money for his brain sickness from using heroin for nineteen years. When the government got a lead that Danny was getting cash money from preaching across the country and world, investigations began. Supposedly, Danny quickly dropped the free mental distress pay he had received for years.

It was noted that Jim Jones had a lot of sexual behavior with his members. Adultery was not preached in his empire, and was not condemned. A young man in Ray's close affiliation, had sex with an underage adopted daughter of his. Early warning was supposedly provided to Ray, but he did nothing until the situation became full blown. The Chief Apostle Ray had no power over the courts and judge, and the young man went to prison. Did the early Apostles, like Peter, or Paul & Silas have power over the jails, and the rulings of the courts?

Both Jim and Ray are guilty of tearing families apart. And both probably did it with twisted scriptures. Jim had a lot of twisted views and many of them were not Bible based. Ray and his other apostles have some strange doctrines that are contradiction to the Bible. This book is meant to warn the reader of the spiritual dangers of this present-day cult. They are spiritually poisoning their members with a false hope of complying with the cult, but in grave danger for what is required to make heaven. You may have friends or family members in it. Maybe you are a member and trying to figure this out spiritually why it is wrong for you to stay. Don't focus on the good corn and oats that they preach. The devil preached a true message to Jesus when he had fasted forty days. But dear reader, focus on the poison that has been presented to you. It might be the only warning you get. Thank you for reading this book. Don't let the contents go void.

www.ingramcontent.com/pod-product-compliance
Lightning Source LLC
Chambersburg PA
CBHW032055040426
42335CB00037B/860